# Fighting Fire
# Fire Safety in Action

by Mari Schuh

**Consulting Editor:** Gail Saunders-Smith, PhD

**Consultant:** Keith S. Frangiamore, Vice President of Operations
Fire Safety Consultants Inc., Elgin, Illinois

Capstone
press

Mankato, Minnesota

Pebble Plus is published by Capstone Press,
151 Good Counsel Drive, P.O. Box 669, Mankato, Minnesota 56002.
www.capstonepress.com

1 2 3 4 5 6 14 13 12 11 10 09

*Library of Congress Cataloging-in-Publication Data*
Schuh, Mari C., 1975–
    Fire safety in action / by Mari Schuh.
    p. cm. — (Pebble plus. Fighting fire)
    Includes bibliographical references and index.
    Summary: "In simple text and photos, provides advice on fire safety" — Provided by publisher.
    ISBN-13: 978-1-4296-1723-9 (hardcover)
    ISBN-10: 1-4296-1723-3 (hardcover)
    1. Fire prevention — Juvenile literature. 2. Fire extinction — Safety measures — Juvenile literature. I. Title.
TH9148.S3795 2009
613.6 — dc22                                                                                     2008026954

**Editorial Credits**
Sarah L. Schuette, editor; Tracy Davies, designer; Marcy Morin, photo shoot scheduler

**Photo Credits**
Capstone Press/Karon Dubke, all

## Note to Parents and Teachers

The Fighting Fire set supports national science standards related to science, technology, and
society. This book describes and illustrates fire safety. The images support early readers in
understanding the text. The repetition of words and phrases helps early readers learn new
words. This book also introduces early readers to subject-specific vocabulary words, which are
defined in the Glossary section. Early readers may need assistance to read some words and to
use the Table of Contents, Glossary, Read More, Internet Sites, and Index
sections of the book.

# Table of Contents

Be Prepared. . . . . . . . . . . . . . . 4

Staying Safe . . . . . . . . . . . . . . 8

Fire Drills . . . . . . . . . . . . . . . 14

A Good Job . . . . . . . . . . . . 20


Glossary . . . . . . . . . . . . . . 22

Read More . . . . . . . . . . . . . 23

Internet Sites. . . . . . . . . . . . 23

Index . . . . . . . . . . . . . . . . . 24

# Be Prepared

Fire gives us heat and light.

But fire is dangerous.

You can learn to be safe around fire.

Look around your home.

Every floor should have

a smoke alarm.

Remind your parents

to test them once a month.

# Staying Safe

Sleep with your bedroom door closed.
The door keeps out smoke and flames if there's a fire.

Have an adult help you cook in the kitchen. Stand away from stoves, grills, and campfires.

Make a map of your house
with your family.
Plan your escape route.

# Fire Drills

Practice a fire drill
with your family
at least once each year.
Crawl low under the smoke
to an exit.

Get out of the building
as fast as you can.
Never go back inside
to get anything.

If your clothes are on fire,

stop, drop, and roll.

Drop to the ground.

Roll around to put out

the flames.

# A Good Job

Fire is fast and hot. Knowing what to do helps you stay safe.

# Glossary

**escape** — to get out of a dangerous situation quickly; it is important to plan ways to escape from your house if it is ever on fire.

**exit** — the door or other way out of a place

**map** — a detailed drawing of a place

**remind** — to help someone remember something

**smoke alarm** — a buzzer or bell that gives a warning; smoke alarms should be tested at least once each year.

# Read More

**Barraclough, Sue**. *Fire Safety*. Stay Safe. Chicago: Heinemann, 2008.

**Rivera, Sheila**. *Fire Safety*. First Step Nonfiction. Minneapolis: Lerner, 2007.

# Internet Sites

FactHound offers a safe, fun way to find educator-approved Internet sites related to this book.

Here's what you do:

1. Visit *www.facthound.com*
2. Choose your grade level.
3. Begin your search.

This book's ID number is 9781429617239.

FactHound will fetch the best sites for you!

# Index

bedroom safety, 8
campfires, 10
cooking, 10
crawling low, 14
escape routes, 12
exits, 14
family, 6, 12, 14
fire drills, 14

grills, 10
heat, 4
light, 4
maps, 12
sleeping, 8
smoke alarms, 6
stop, drop, and roll, 18
stoves, 10

Word Count: 155
Grade: 1
Early-Intervention Level: 18